101 THANKSGIVING KNOCK-KNOCKS, JOKES, AND RIDDLES

by Suzanne Lord
illustrated by Don Orehek

SCHOLASTIC INC.
New York Toronto London Auckland Sydney

ISBN 0-590-47163-5

12 11 10 9 8 7 6 5 4 3 2 1   3 4 5 6 7 8/9

Printed in the U.S.A.   01

First Scholastic printing, October 1993

To turkeys everywhere!

THANK GOODNESS
FOR THANKSGIVING!

Ivan: If twenty Thanksgiving turkeys told terrible tales, how many "t's" would there be in all?

Carl: Seven?

Ivan: Gotcha! None—there are no "t's" in the word *all*.

If April showers bring May flowers,
what do May flowers bring?

Pilgrims!

5

SILLY SHOPPING

A lady went to the store and bought a bag of potatoes. An hour later she was back in the store, furious.

"You told me that this bag of potatoes was mold free," she fumed at the store clerk. "Just look at them—they're practically green! How could you lie to me like that?"

"I'm no liar," the clerk replied. "I didn't charge you a penny for that mold. It was free!"

Dad: Where can I find a great turkey?
Clerk: Wherever you left it, I guess.

A newlywed went to the store to buy her first Thanksgiving turkey. As she paid for it, she asked, "Do you know how long turkeys are supposed to be cooked?"

The store owner thought for a minute and then told her, "As long as short ones, I imagine."

PILGRIM GRINS

Pilgrim 1: What dost thou? 'Tis a weekday and thou workest not?

Pilgrim 2: Indeed not. For I am a candle-maker, and I am hired to work only on *wick*-ends.

Pilgrim John: I see thee cleaning hunting gear for the morrow. Dost thou plan on hunting bear?

Pilgrim Samuel: Certainly not, John, and I am shocked that thou would suggest it! I shall wear clothing as usual.

Pilgrim William: Why did Pilgrim James eat a candle, pray tell?
Pilgrim Daniel: I understand he was not very hungry and only wanted a light snack.

GOBBLER GIGGLES

Jane: What's a baby turkey called?
Joan: I don't know. What?
Jane: A peeping Tom.

Sally: What do you call a turkey who's fallen into a muddy pool?

Dan: A murky turkey. What do you call an excited turkey?

Sally: That's too easy. A perky turkey! What do you get when you have a turkey on the beach with Broomhilda?

Dan: You've got me. What's that?

Sally: A turkey sand-*witch*!

Joe: What do you get when you cross a turkey with a banjo?

Moe: I don't know. What?

Joe: A turkey that plucks himself!

MORE SILLY SHOPPING

A man went to get a turkey from a live poultry farm. "Do you have any turkeys going cheap?" he asked.

"Nope," said the owner. "All our turkeys go 'gobble, gobble.'"

Ruth was frantic. "Hurry up, Nellie! You've been in the store forever. If you don't hurry we'll be late for Thanksgiving dinner."

Nellie just smiled. "Don't worry," she said. "We can't be late."

"How can you say that?" Ruth asked. "Dinner is supposed to start in fifteen minutes!"

"I've got the turkey," Nellie replied smugly.

Mom went to the store looking for fresh cranberries. The ones she found looked terrible. "Don't you have any better berries than these?" she asked the clerk.

"Lady, that's all we've got," the clerk snapped.

"But these cranberries are old and dried and wrinkled!"

"So?" the clerk bit back. "Serve 'em as *gran*-berries."

"Marcia, would you like some popcorn?"

"Not really. My dad just yelled at me, and I'm too mad to eat popcorn. Could I have some *mom*-corn instead, please?"

Louie: Last Thanksgiving I made popcorn over a roaring fire, and my parents got really angry at me.

Lizzie: Why?

Louie: I guess because we don't have a fireplace.

"What does your dad do?" asked Lou.

"My dad's a magician," Mike replied. "Every day he turns our car into the driveway!"

"My dad's a taxi driver," said Lou. "He makes money by driving his customers away."

"Say, Mackie," Mike asked, "why are you looking so glum?"

"My dad's an archaeologist," Mackie answered, "and his entire career is in ruins!"

Billy: I can't wait to go to Grandma's for Thanksgiving. My cousin's going to be there, and he has three feet!

Willie: Wow — how'd that happen?

Billy: I don't know. My aunt wrote my parents and said, "You won't recognize little Howard — he's grown another foot!"

"I'm confused," Alice said. "You say you both have the same parents, you both look exactly alike, but you say you're not twins. How can that be?"

Jim and Tim smiled and answered, "You haven't met Slim—we're triplets!"

Alma: Are the pig people coming this Thanksgiving?

Dad: Who are the pig people?

Alma: Aunt Helen and Uncle Bob.

Dad: Whatever gave you the idea to call them pig people?

Alma: You. Last year you said that Aunt Helen was a crashing boar, and Uncle Bob was a ham!

A TRULY OLD JOKE

Harriet: Do you know how to make a turkey float?

Nanny: No, dear. How do you do that?

Harriet: Put the turkey in a glass with cola and ice cream.

A little girl walked into a meat store and said, "I'd like a turkey for my grandma."

"Sorry," replied the clerk. "We don't do exchanges."

Gwen: We had my grandma and grandpa from Detroit for Thanksgiving dinner last year.

Ronny: Really? We had turkey and dressing.

THANKSGIVING COOKING CHUCKLES

Jimmy: Mmmmm. That turkey smells good and it's not even done yet. How long will it be?

Mom: About the same length as it was before I put it into the oven, I suppose.

"Every year there's not enough stuffing," Jennie complained. "But this year I've figured out how to make the stuffing last."

"What are you going to do?" asked Penny.

"Make everything else first!" Jennie said proudly.

Mom asked little Mary to mix the cake batter. When Mary got to the part that said "separate two eggs," she put one on the front porch and one on the back porch.

MORE PILGRIM GRINS

Mistress Samantha: I'm at my wit's
end. Our rooster will not crow.

Mistress Wynne: What a pity. No
cock-a-doodle-do in the morning?

Mistress Samantha: No, I'm afraid
our rooster is a cock-a-doodle-don't.

Pilgrim 1: Why dost thou have two
blunderbusses to shoot game with?

Pilgrim 2: I often miss the first time.
With the second blunderbuss, I usu-
ally hit my mark.

Pilgrim 1: Why not use the second gun
first, so thou wilt not miss!

DON'T KNOCK THANKSGIVING

Knock, knock.
Who's there?
Donna Mae Kew.
Donna Mae Kew who?
Donna Mae Kew the best dinner you've
    ever had!

Knock, knock.

Who's there?

Harry.

Harry who?

Harry up. I'm starved!

Knock, knock.
Who's there?
Abbott.
Abbott who?
Abbott time to eat, isn't it?

Knock, knock.
Who's there?
Dewey.
Dewey who?
Dewey have to wait long to eat?

Knock, knock.
Who's there?
Diana.
Diana who?
Diana thirst, too.

LET'S EAT

Kate: I'm so hungry, I can describe my stomach in two letters.
Earl: Which two?
Kate: M-T.

Mom went to get her fresh baked rolls from the oven. They were burned to a crisp.

"My rolls are ruined!" she cried. "Jimmy, didn't I tell you to watch these rolls and notice when they were getting too brown?"

"Yes, ma'am," Jimmy said proudly, "and I did. They were too brown about half an hour ago."

Mom: At our house we always say a prayer before we eat.

Aunt: Sis, if you still cook the way you did when we were younger, they *should* pray!

"Where are you going, young lady?"

"To the dinner table."

"Not with dirty hands."

"No, ma'am. I'm going with Cousin Jerry."

Trevor: Were these cranberries shipped here from Maine?
Uncle Gus: I believe they were.
Tevor: Then I guess they came by *cran*-ferry.

Pam: Have some can-berries.
Olga: Don't you mean cranberries?
Pam: Nope. These came out of a can.

WHAT NOT TO SAY TO A TURKEY ON THE DAY BEFORE THANKSGIVING

- Gosh, Tom, you look good enough to eat.
- You'll laugh your head off when you hear this.
- Let's bury the hatchet, shall we?
- Don't lose your head over it.

TURKEY RIDDLES

What goes "gobble, gobble" and can see just as well from one end as from the other?

A turkey with his eyes shut.

What goes "gobble, gobble, BOOM"?

A turkey in a mine field.

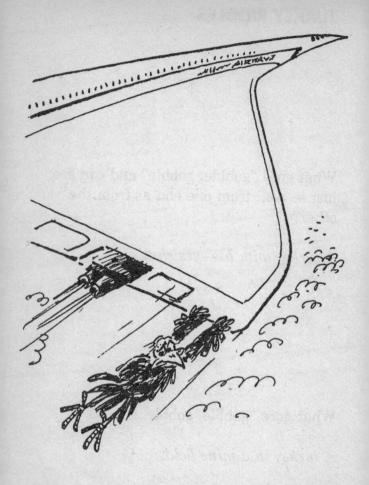

What goes "gobble, gobble" and flies at two thousand miles per hour?

A turkey on the Concorde.

What goes "gobble, gobble, ha-ha-ha, BOOM"?

A turkey exploding with laughter.

What goes "gobble, gobble, ha-ha-ha, PLOP"?

A turkey laughing his head off.

Where are most turkeys found?

Between the head and the tail.

What do you call a turkey farm the day before Thanksgiving?

A chop shop.

Why is a couch like a turkey?

Because they're both full of stuffing.

Why did the turkey chick bolt down his food?

Because he was a little gobbler.

Why is a turkey on Thanksgiving like a ghost the day after Halloween?

Because he's gone today, but just the day before he was a-gobblin'.

Why was the turkey wearing pink sneakers?

Because his boots were being repaired.

Grandpa: What's this?
Grandma: It's bean soup.
Grandpa: I don't care what it's been.
   What is it now?

Sonny: Is Grandpa Jones a baker?
Mom: Why, yes, Sonny.
Sonny: Then he must be really rich!
Mom: What makes you say that?
Sonny: He's always got plenty of
  dough.

Sue: Do you know why the turkey
  crossed the road?
Drew: No. Why?
Sue: To prove he wasn't chicken.

Grandma: What would you like for dessert, Joey?

Joey: Pumpkin pie!

Grandma: Pumpkin pie, what, dear? Say the magic word.

Joey: I'm sorry, Grandma—pumpkin pie, abracadabra!

Roger: Are your grandparents alive?

Barry: Yep. In fact, they're living at a hundred twenty-five.

Roger: What? That's impossible!

Barry: Not at all. They're living at 125 Maple Drive.

"Betty, didn't we have a big talk about give and take?"

"Yes, Dad."

"Then why did you hit your cousin and eat his dessert?"

"I did just like you said, Dad. I gave him a punch in the nose and took his dessert."

Just as the Thanksgiving meal was about to be served, Dan tripped on the rug and dropped a tray full of turkey.

"Gosh, that reminds me. I have to do a history paper," said Jimmy.

"What's it about?" asked Dan.

"The fall of Turkey."

Mom: Donny, why aren't you eating any stuffing tonight?

Donnie: What's the use of eating any stuffing tonight when the bully down the block is going to knock it out of me tomorrow?

THANKSGIVING DINNER RIDDLES

What's full of raisins and is on a secret mission?

Mince spy.

What's red, round, and goes up and down, up and down?

A cranberry on an elevator.

What's orange and falls off walls?

Humpty Pumpkin.

What's round, red, and attracted to metal objects?

A magnetic cranberry.

What's round, red, and shocking?

An electric cranberry.

MORE DON'T KNOCK THANKSGIVING

Knock, knock.
Who's there?
Sid.
Sid who?
Sid down. It's time to eat.

Knock, knock.
Who's there?
Luke.
Luke who?
Luke at all the food!

Knock, knock.

Who's there?

Odette.

Odette who?

Odette's a big turkey.

Knock, knock.
Who's there?
Philippa.
Philippa who?
Philippa plate and dig in.

Knock, knock.
Who's there?
Phyllis.
Phyllis who?
Phyllis plate up, too, please!

Knock, knock.
Who's there?
Buddha.
Buddha who?
Buddha my roll, please.

Knock, knock.
Who's there?
Emma.
Emma who?
Emma real pig when it comes to turkey.

Knock, knock.
Who's there?
Olive.
Olive who?
Olive the stuffing, too!

Knock, knock.
Who's there?
Aaron.
Aaron who?
Aaron you having any more cranberry
     sauce?

Knock, knock.
Who's there?
Anita.
Anita who?
Anita nother napkin.

Tom Turkey: You look battered and
bruised. What happened?

Turkey Lurkey: I'm not sure. There
were a lot of men in the woods, and
every time one of them called for
Tim, a tree would fall on me.

Tom Turkey: Who is Tim?

Turkey Lurkey: I never saw him, but
I'll never forget his name—*Tim
Burr*!

"Poor old Tom," Turkey Lurkey sighed. "The other day he was just a turkey in the straw. Then the farmer axed him, the farmer's wife plucked him, and he was turkey in the raw. Now he's been cooked for Thanksgiving, and he'll be turkey inside Pa."

What did John Alden wear on his feet?

Plymouth socks.

What kind of music did Pilgrims listen to?

Plymouth rock.

How did Pilgrims know what time it was?

Plymouth clocks.

What did Priscilla Alden comb at night?

Her Plymouth locks.

GRANDSON OF
RELATIVELY SPEAKING

Uncle Ted: Kenny, you look terrible.
Did you have an accident?

Kenny: No, it wasn't any accident. It
was my cousin Sid, and he meant
every minute of it.

Aunt Betty: You don't like my pie? Why, I've been making mince pies since before you were born, young man.

Denny: Oh, that explains it. This must be one of them.

EVEN MORE
DON'T KNOCK THANKSGIVING

Knock, knock.
Who's there?
Esther.
Esther who?
Esther any more gravy?

Knock, knock.
Who's there?
Arthur.
Arthur who?
Arthur any more sweet potatoes?

Knock, knock.
Who's there?
Don.
Don who?
Don eat all the stuffing. I want some
   more!

Knock, knock.
Who's there?
Wanda.
Wanda who?
Wanda piece of pumpkin pie?

Knock, knock.
Who's there?
Alma.
Alma who?
Alma dinner's gone. Can I have dessert?

Knock, knock.
Who's there?
Alva.
Alva who?
Alva 'nother piece, please.

Knock, knock.
Who's there?
Xavier.
Xavier who?
Xavier fork for dessert.

Knock, knock.
Who's there?
Norma Lee.
Norma Lee who?
Norma Lee I don't eat this much.

Knock, knock.
Who's there?
General Lee.
General Lee who?
General Lee, neither do I.

Knock, knock.

Who's there?

Aida.

Aida who?

Aida lot more than I should have.

Knock, knock.
Who's there?
Tamara.
Tamara who?
Tamara we'll have turkey hash.

Knock, knock.
Who's there?
Gladys.
Gladys who?
Gladys Thanksgiving, aren't you?

TALKING TURKEY

Kyle: Why did the turkey flock go to the park?

Kevin: For their own fowl purposes?

Kyle: No! For fowl play.

Kevin: Did they play fowl ball?

Kyle: Yes, and it was a wild game!

What's the best way to catch a turkey?

Have someone throw one at you.

Which side of the turkey has the most feathers?

The outside.

RELATIVELY SPEAKING—
THE FINAL CHAPTER

Aunt Bertha: Well, little Danny, I'm going now. Are you disappointed?
Danny: You bet! I thought you'd be gone two hours ago!

Aunt Betty: Nobody does any work around here but me! I suppose I have to put the coffee on myself, too.

Ginny: Gosh, no, Aunt Betty. You can put it on the table.

THANKSGIVING—THE TAIL END

Fran: What always comes at the end of Thanksgiving?
Gwen: Football?
Fran: Nope—the letter "G."

SEE YOU NEXT YEAR!

After Thanksgiving dinner was over, Mort saw his little brother Sid in the backyard, poking holes in the dirt and filling them with birdseed.

"Why are you planting birdseed?" Mort asked.

"I'm growing next year's turkey," Sid replied.